Air Pow

MW00846263

MH-53E
SEA DRAGON

MEGAN COOLEY PETERSON

BLACK
RABBIT
BOOKS

Bolt is published by Black Rabbit Books
P.O. Box 3263, Mankato, Minnesota, 56002.
www.blackrabbitbooks.com
Copyright © 2020 Black Rabbit Books

Jennifer Besel & Marysa Storm, editors;
Grant Gould, designer; Omay Ayres,
photo researcher

All rights reserved. No part of this book may be reproduced, stored in a
retrieval system or transmitted in any form or by any means, electronic,
mechanical, photocopying, recording, or otherwise, without written
permission from the publisher.

Library of Congress Cataloging-in-Publication Data
Names: Peterson, Megan Cooley, author.
Title: MH-53E Sea Dragon / by Megan Cooley Peterson.
Description: Mankato, Minnesota : Black Rabbit Books, [2020] | Series:
Bolt. Air Power | Includes bibliographical references and index.
Identifiers: LCCN 2018033588 (print) | LCCN 2018035230 (ebook) |
ISBN 9781680727951 (e-book) | ISBN 9781680727890 (library binding) |
ISBN 9781644660126 (paperback)
Subjects: LCSH: Sikorsky H-53 (Military transport helicopter)—
Juvenile literature.
Classification: LCC UG1232.T72 (ebook) | LCC UG1232.T72 P48 2020
(print) | DDC 623.74/65—dc23
LC record available at https://lccn.loc.gov/2018033588

Printed in the United States. 1/19

Image Credits

Alamy: Military Collection, Cover; PJF Mil-
itary Collection, 16; PR Collection, 26–27; RGB
Ventures / SuperStock, 5, 22; army.mil: Pfc. Deomontez
Duncan/US Army, 25; commons.wikimedia.org: Scott Shea,
13 (t); commons.wikimedia.org/navy.mil: Capt. Paul Duncan/
US Navy, 1; Photographer's Mate 2nd Class Michael J. Sandberg/
US Navy, 3, 26 (t); United States of America MC3 Taylor N. Stinson/
US Navy, 10; commons.wikimedia.org/navy/mil: Mass Communication
Specialist 2nd Class Dustin Kelling/US Navy, 15; editart.club: Dabarti, 4;
navair.navy.mil: US Navy, 8–9; navy.mil: Mass Communication Specialist
2nd Class Michael Bevan/US Navy, 6; Mass Communication Specialist 2nd
Class Patrick A. Ratcliff/US Navy, 22; Mass Communication Specialist 3rd
Class Sean Galbreath/US Navy, 24; Petty Officer 3rd Class Joshua M. Tol-
bert/US Navy, 27 (b); Photographers Mate 2nd Class Daniel J. McLain, 31;
Senior Chief Mass Communication Specialist Joe Kane/US Navy, 28–29;
Senior Chief Naval Aircrewman (Helicopter) Josh Husband/US Navy, 13
(br); US Navy, 12–13 (bkgd), 32; seaforces.org: US Navy, 12 (both),
13 (bl); Shutterstock: inspired-fiona, 19 (bkgd); turbosquid.com:
3dshtorm, 20–21; vi.m.wikipedia.org: Jetijones, 19 (art)
Every effort has been made to contact copyright holders for
material reproduced in this book. Any omissions will
be rectified in subsequent printings if notice is
given to the publisher.

CONTENTS

CHAPTER 1

Keeping the
Waters Safe............4

CHAPTER 2

History of the
Sea Dragon............8

CHAPTER 3

Sea Dragon Features...14

CHAPTER 4

The Sea Dragon
in Action..............23

Other Resources..........30

Keeping the Waters

A Sea Dragon helicopter flies above the ocean. It drags a **minesweeping** sled over the water. Soldiers in the chopper are looking for underwater **mines**. The sled will find dangerous areas.

Explosion

Soon, the soldiers find a mine. The sled safely sets it off. Water explodes into the air. Soldiers in the Sea Dragon continue the search. They won't stop until the waters are safe.

The Sea Dragon is a powerful helicopter. Its main mission is to find and destroy mines.

The chopper is sometimes used to deliver supplies. It can also be used during battles.

CHAPTER 2

HISTORY
of the Sea Dragon

In the 1980s, the U.S. Navy wanted a new helicopter. It needed to be able to find underwater mines. The Navy turned to a helicopter called the Super Stallion. The Stallion could lift heavy things. The Navy needed its power.

**The chopper can fly 885 miles
(1,425 kilometers) without refueling.**

New Features and a New Name

The Navy made some changes to the Stallion. Engineers added larger fuel tanks. The new chopper could carry an extra 1,000 gallons (3,785 liters) of fuel. With extra fuel, the chopper could fly longer. They also gave it **towing** equipment. Then they named it the MH-53E Sea Dragon.

June
1986
The chopper is **combat** ready.

1980

December 23,
1981
The Sea Dragon
takes its first flight.

1991
Sea Dragons destroy
underwater mines
near Kuwait.

2020

2012
They hunt for
underwater mines
in the Middle East.

2017
They bring aid to Puerto
Rico after a hurricane.

13

CHAPTER 3

Sea Dragon

FEATURES

The Sea Dragon is one of the largest military helicopters. It weighs 36,745 pounds (16,667 kilograms) empty. It can carry up to 55 soldiers.

MAXIMUM WEIGHT AT TAKEOFF

Super Stallion

Sea Dragon

Osprey

Black Hawk

maximum weight   10,000

73,500 pounds (33,339 kg)

69,750 pounds (31,638 kg)

52,600 pounds (23,859 kg)

22,000 pounds (9,979 kg)

| 20,000 | 30,000 | 40,000 | 50,000 | 60,000 | 70,000 | 80,000 |

Minesweeping Sleds

AQS-14A	Uses **sonar** to find and explode mines.
MK 103	Cuts mines tied to the ocean floor.
MK 104	Uses sound waves to blow up mines.
MK 105	Blows up mines using magnets.

Minesweeping

The Sea Dragon pulls minesweeping sleds. Each sled has a different job. Magnets on the Mk 105 sled blow up mines. The sled weighs about 8,000 pounds (3,629 kg).

Rotors and Speed

The Sea Dragon has two **rotors**. The main rotor has seven blades. The tail rotor has four blades. Rotors allow the helicopter to **hover**. The Sea Dragon can fly up to 173 miles (278 km) per hour.

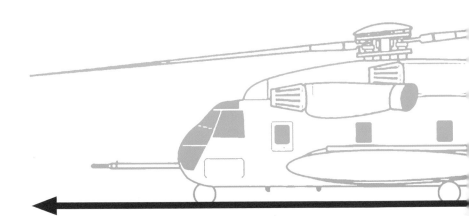

height
28.3 feet (8.6 meters)

SEA DRAGON STATS

rotor diameter
79 feet (24 m)

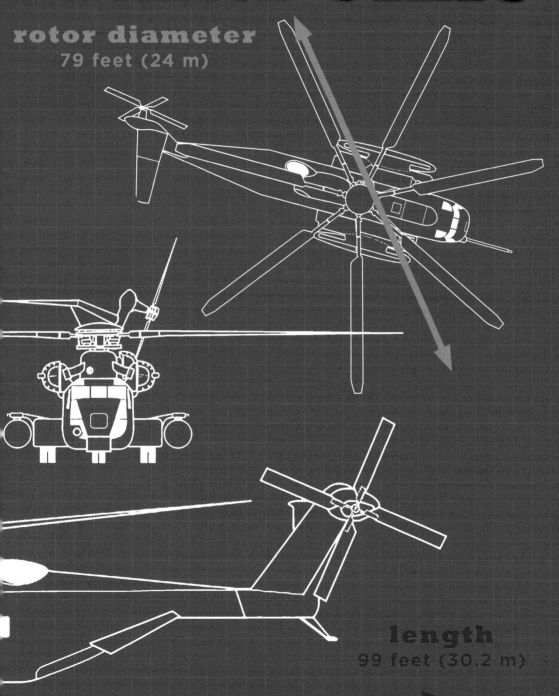

length
99 feet (30.2 m)

SEA DRAGON PARTS

TAIL ROTOR

MACHINE GUN
(CAN BE MOUNTED
ON REAR RAMP)

CABIN

MAIN ROTOR

COCKPIT

The helicopters did 57 hours of drills.

CHAPTER 4

The Sea Dragon in ACTION

Sea Dragon pilots must stay prepared. In 2017, they did training drills in South Korea. They practiced blowing up mines.

Helping Out

Sea Dragons also bring supplies to people in need. A hurricane hit Puerto Rico in 2017. The storm caused a lot of damage. Sea Dragons brought food and water. They also carried concrete barriers to fix a broken dam.

BY THE NUMBERS

2
NUMBER OF PILOTS NEEDED TO FLY A SEA DRAGON

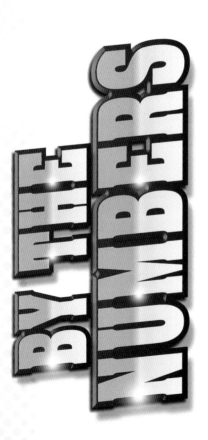

10,000 feet
(3,048 m)
MAXIMUM HEIGHT THE CHOPPER CAN FLY

32,000
pounds (14,515 kg)

AMOUNT OF CARGO
THE CHOPPER
CAN CARRY

10,000 HOURS

time a Sea Dragon
can fly before
it's retired

Important Missions

Sea Dragons are used for many jobs. They explode underwater mines before they hurt people. They also bring supplies to places in need. This powerful chopper does important work.

It is the only U.S. military chopper that can be used to find mines.

GLOSSARY

cargo (KAR-go)—something carried from one place to another

combat (kahm-BAT)—active fighting, often in a war

hover (HUHV-er)—floating in the air without moving any direction

mine (MYN)—an explosive in the ground or in water that is set to explode when disturbed

minesweeping (MYN-sweep-ing)—finding and destroying mines by dragging

retire (ree-TIYR)—to withdraw from use

rotor (RO-tuhr)—spinning blades that support a helicopter in the air

sonar (SOH-nar)—a device that uses sound waves to find objects underwater

towing (TOH-ing)—able to pull along behind

BOOKS

Garstecki, Julia. *Military Aircraft.* Military Tech. Mankato, MN: Black Rabbit Books, 2018.

Kiland, Taylor Baldwin, and Karen and Glen Bledsoe. *Military Helicopters: Heroes of the Sky.* Military Engineering in Action. New York: Enslow Publishing, 2016.

Nagelhout, Ryan. *Military Helicopters.* Mighty Military Machines. New York: Gareth Stevens Publishing, 2015.

WEBSITES

MH-53 Boat Landing
www.youtube.com/watch?v=AZV6LCLKRgU

MH-53E Sea Dragon
www.navair.navy.mil/index.cfm?fuseaction=home. displayplatform&key=51a3587e-c772-4adc-8197- 4f4fe69216bb

MH-53E Sea Dragon Helicopter
www.navy.mil/navydata/fact_display. asp?cid=1200&tid=400&ct=1

INDEX

C

crews, 23, 26

F

features, 11, 18, 20–21

H

history, 8, 11, 12–13

M

minesweeping sleds,
    4, 7, 16, 17

missions, 4, 7, 12–13,
    24, 29

R

ranges, 10

S

sizes, 14, 18–19

speeds, 18

W

weapons, 20

weight, 14–15, 27